THE WATERMARK

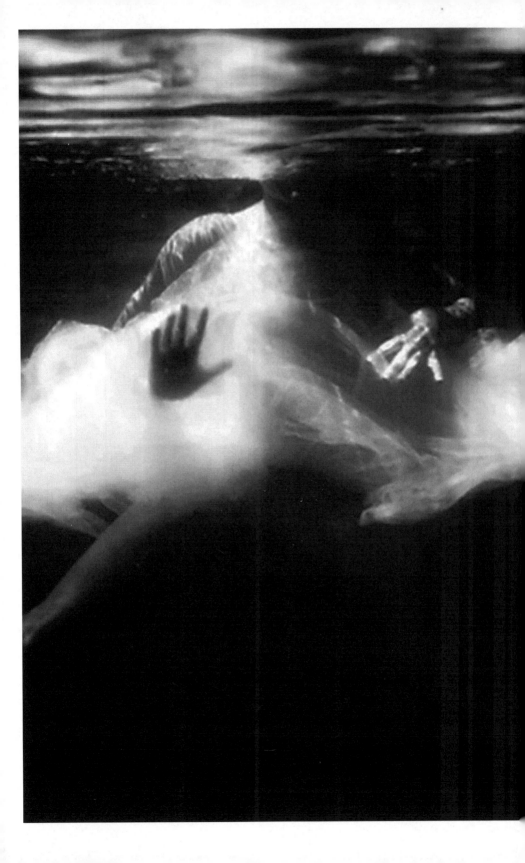

THE
WATERMARK
ALICE ANDERSON

EYEWEAR PUBLISHING

First published in 2016
by Eyewear Publishing Ltd
Suite 333, 19-21 Crawford Street
Marylebone, London W1H 1PJ
United Kingdom

Cover design and typeset by Edwin Smet
Cover photograph by Elena Kalis
Printed in England by TJ International Ltd, Padstow, Cornwall

The right of Alice Anderson to be identified as author of
this work has been asserted in accordance with section 77
of the Copyright, Designs and Patents Act 1988

ISBN 978-1-911335-20-7

*Eyewear wishes to thank Jonathan Wonham for his
generous patronage of our press.*

*The editor has generally followed American spelling and punctuation
at the author's request.*

WWW.EYEWEARPUBLISHING.COM

Alice Anderson
is the author of *Human Nature: Poems*,
awarded both the Best First Book Prize from
the Great Lakes Colleges Association and the Elmer
Holmes Bobst Prize for Emerging Writers from NYU.
Anderson holds an MFA from Sarah Lawrence College,
and her memoir, *Some Bright Morning I'll Fly Away*, was
sold at auction to St. Martin's Press. With work appearing
in journals such as *New Letters*, *CUTTHROAT*, *The New
York Quarterly*, *Tupelo Quarterly*, and *AGNI*. Anderson is
anthologized in *On The Verge: Emerging Poets and Artists;
American Poetry, The Next Generation;* and in the 20th
anniversary edition of the classic, *The Courage to Heal*.
Anderson has been a visiting poet at Kenyon College, Hope
College, St. Mary's College, Oberlin, and others.
The recipient of a prestigious Haven Foundation
grant for writers recovering from Traumatic Brain
Injury, Anderson lives in Sacramento, and is
currently at work on a third poetry
collection and a novel.

TABLE OF CONTENTS

IV. Paper Sack of Majesty

A Wounded Deer—leaps highest

– Emily Dickinson

I

Joy Ride

THE WATER

In memory: 238 dead, 67 missing Mississippians who stayed, August 29, 2005.

*Hurricane Katrina made its final landfall near the Mississippi/Louisiana
state line, sustaining winds of 120 mph. A commanding 27-foot storm surge
penetrated six miles inland on land and up to 12 miles inland (maintaining
its brutal 27-foot surge) in bays, rivers, inlets, and bayous.*

She comes in quick, after the wind. She comes a towering
          fortress of exactitude, her skirts
gathered up then let loose around her in the terrible
          swirling fais do-do.

She is all stirred up and been drinking since dawn. She comes
          in with the darkness but
she's not ashamed, nor hiding, nor subtle. She is
          tall as the day is long and

her breasts leak with the searching hungry mouths of
          greedy little boys always
underfoot. The water is wide, her hips slap against
          the doorway to your

entire life. She engulfs you like an orgasm that
          won't ever quit, her wet excess
going and going and going, breathing, alive with electricity,
          like the sharpness

of a slap on sunburned skin. She rattles the pilings and
          scoops up the boats, she is
whoring with the water moccasins and devouring
          the cats. And the squirrels

and the rats and the possom and the god-awful
          please-shoot-em-dollar-a-tail nutria
we were trying to be rid of in the anyhow. The dead beasts
          turn in an ornate

concoction within her and become the punctuation
          in the alphabet of sticks
which used to be the buildings of this town. The birds have
          all flown away.

The water is your lover and your end. She is inescapable, sweet
          as King Cake and three times
as festive. Baby Jesus spirals in her roiling destruction
          like a child swaddled

in nothing at all. She's kicking it up with confusion, not sure
          if she's to scratch her watch
or wind her ass, but happy to have caused
          a commotion.

She is the new creation, remaking every surface with
          her slate gray fate.
Her desire thrums like a motorboat's engine on a fine summer
          day. She's a silver tea service

guest in every home, she rips the rug from the floors
          and the leaves from every
branch. She's greedy, and pretty, and loud. When she
          arrives at the mausoleum

she slinks into every last crevice and sucks the dead out
          with her when she goes.
When the water goes she goes without pause. No time
          to waste. She rushes back

into evening like a train on a switch, a girl thrown from
        a high rise, soiled water slipping down a wide-open drain.
She leaves the beaches littered: deep freezes empty of fish,
        splintered hulls of party

boats, shards of china and brick, dead bodies ripped nude
        of their Sunday funeral best, shoes and
toys and tires and shovelheads and lawn mowers, ten thousand
        formerly frozen

rotting chicken carcasses, fat playground elephants up-ended
        from their rusty springs, blankets
in branches, a vast expanse of Styrofoam beer coolers with
        no one come to the fete.

She is death or desire, one.
She is death and desire, both.

She comes in and takes you like a lover, swift and fierce
        and seemingly devoted,
and takes all your money and your children
        when she goes.

THE QUIET

Ocean Springs, Mississippi, August 30, 2005, the day after Katrina made landfall.

A nutria is an approximately twelve-pound, furry, armadillo-like semi-aquatic rodent, the female possessing multiple breasts on her sides so her young can suckle while she floats down quiet bayous, inlets, and canals.

She comes slinking in late for the party, empty-handed and all dolled up
in a soiled taffeta dress. She finds you sleeping, nude on the slab, and licks

with her mossy boozy tongue the length of your grimy thigh. She's
one of those girls who lies down drunk in a big windy swish on your

divan and that's the end of that and you ain't never getting her out.
She comes in after the freight train roar of the storm surge, after

the water with her slapping hips and grand castle of meticulousness
has had her way with it all. She is the water's little sister, not quite

as pretty, but three times as stubborn with something to prove. She
comes in quiet, like prayer. She can't make a preacher cuss, can't make him

speak in tongues, but she is the new truth—the word, etched into every
drenched surface, never uttered aloud. She tiptoes in while the grown-ups

fight, like a pregnant teenager through an evening window, out past curfew
and tipping over the sill. The quiet slaps the hand of snickering

children and smothers the mouths of fucking lovers with her palm.
You cannot escape her. She is obliteration in a see-through chemise.

When the quiet comes, she's hungry, and even after she's gobbled up
the birds, their wee petite wings crispy in her teeth, even after she's sipped

the pulp of every last dragonfly and supped up the oil off every drowned
cat, she still holds a twin set of muddy god-damn-Uncle-Poot-shot-enough-to-

score-a-twelve-pack nutria females under the bathwater, their rubbery
tails knocking suds over the edge, sopping her scabby knees, until they're

quiet, until they float one last time. And then she eats them, too. The quiet
is satisfied with nothing less than oblivion: she shushes the babies and

stifles the wives. She is a husband's raised hand and the sting that won't
settle on a porcelain cheek. She yanks and twists the royal blue robes up

over the heads and into the mouths of the choir. She is the new
hymn, exalting her praise to destruction. She is your daily chorus, endlessly

repeating. You'll never forget her song. No place to rest in the quiet.
She's the ice box stopped, the leaf blower come to heavenly conclusion.

She's got Michael Chertoff by the shirt collar and she's bound him with violet
feather boas before stuffing him into a FEMA trailer back closet and turning

the lock. She's the opposite of birdsong, enemy of buzz, she's pulled
the tongues from thirty-two miles of lost dogs wandering the coast.

She snakes through the leafless trees and the cracked carcass of what
used to be your home. The quiet, she's a breeze—buck naked, with

15

nothing to strum. She's the moment before the moment, right before
the power comes back and the breaker explodes. She's leaking into every

broken-up waterlogged surface of your life, leaking like the breasts
of your daughter's best friend's mother. The quiet wasn't there as

the family axed through the third story rooftop. The quiet doesn't care
they held on six hours to a tree. She only showed up the next day,

sauntering in to the room when Baby, their smallest boy, died of water
poisoning when no one was looking. The quiet leaks warm milky rivulets on

the mourning mother's borrowed dress. She's there in the eyes of the
sister, she's there in the frost of the morgue. No one gets buried in the quiet,

while the earth is too sodden, the mausoleums have been reduced
to silty piles of marble and bone. She's the sadness, the nonsense

lullaby, she's the funeral hush. She promenades by, rips down your
Don't Loot I'll Shoot sign, puts your pistol in your mama's lace brassiere.

She is calm and catastrophe, one.
She is calm and catastrophe, both.

She comes in an unspoken promise, that girl, after the surge, and wraps
her slight thighs around your hips and she hangs on tight, bucking up

against every bright moment of your devastation. The quiet is your
confirmation. She's set you down on a life of broken glass, and she loves

your bare feet. The quiet comes, wrapping her aching body around
you, her budlike breasts pushing up against your lungs, tickling

and moistening the skin of your ear with her terrible, silent
tongue. Finally, whispering, *Dance, pretty girl, dance.*

The quiet is your unrequited lover, come finally
to take you: a gun to your throat, a diamond ring

in her mouth. She locks your thighs in her ghastly grip,
and never stops kissing you while she fucks.

BIRDS

Two weeks after the storm
driving west

from Ocean Springs to
New Orleans

the baby points his
little crooked finger

to the window,
says,

Look Mama! Black trees!

at what are not black
but instead completely

barren trees—
still standing

without leaves.
Full up thick

with vultures
black

as funeral
shoes. You must

find grace within
the calamity—

that's where all
the beauty

lives.

INTERFERENCE

Tanagers have a naughty reputation
as ravenous, brazen fruit eaters: thieves.
But the Green Honeykeepers hanging
upside down in the neighbor boy's
pink Camellia use their specialized tongues
to suck only the most luscious nectar
from the blooms. Out there all alone,
the neighbor boy—his cheeks smacked crimson
with constellations of freckles. He carves
a Japanese Maple with a switchblade; tapes up
a black Labrador; digs a ravine and pees
a marshland of urine (nails and pennies and
scabs and toy cars rotting in the bottom silt).

Every day: the tree, the dog, the piss.

I want to take him in, keep him until the streetlights
go out. Make cornbread and honey, brush stickers
from his hair, tell him a story about the place between
resilience and stupidity. I want to take him in but he's
already gone now. Only a poster on the tree
and the Honeycreepers hanging tail side up, sounding
their "tchit tchit tchit tchit tchit tchit tchit" alarm, remain.

A man with sinister intentions jumped my sweet gun.

WARRANT

1.

She has a warrant out for her arrest.

The silvery points
of steel badges all
point in her direction—spears
of light, of grace,
of terror.

Her fever warms
the concrete, her fear
sets stop signs afire.
When a doorbell
rings, she thinks,
Small window.
When a siren calls, she hears

Love
Struck,
Love Struck,
Love
Struck.

Please be informed: her heart is steeled, not stolen.

2.
At the card-table security check
of Courthouse A (on the Pascagoula
Fairgrounds, FEMA trailers
like minty Mexican chewing gum squares

tossed in the dirt) the bailiff, a
wiry old gentleman with silver-sky
pompadour, steel-eyes like
a Sunday morning
storm, nods. She unzips
and pulls open for him
her best pocketbook.
His hands flip through: Palmer
brush, powder compact, King
James abbreviated, Revlon
Bed of Roses, and one inky,
loaded Baby Eagle 9mm.

The bailiff smiles, winks, leans
across the listing table, dry lips
whispering in her ear:

Babydoll, I reckon' you left your
eyeglasses
in your car.

JOY RIDE

"No More Joy for Teen": *New Orleans Times Picayune* headline

You put the key in the slot and you turn, igniting the night air with
fumes, the Buick oiled black with twenty years of misuse on back roads

and bayous. No see-ums spin and jerk in the columns of headlight, which
point straight to the interstate. You are fourteen, everything a possibility,

nothing for sure. For now it is midnight, the lunar eclipse, your fight-wearied
parents are fast asleep. Who knows how you know how to do it, how to

ease into drive, push on the gas, and go. But you do it, and black grace
hurtles you out: you're gone. The Buick rocks along, a humid room of

Juicy Fruit breath, brittle leather chirping like bed springs, slick green
dash light filming every surface of metal and glass and skin. The night

is cool, gulf breeze edging off tops of salt pine savannas, edging in to
velvety magnolia buds closed tight, waiting to bloom. You cross the

bridge at Lake Pontchartrain, the stone and white steel pulled taut across
flat water, see ghost fisherman along the pier, gathered around a fire

with all the people they loved once on this earth. You drive and know
the world can be made over in your mind, in an instant, made over slick

like sunset postcards sent from seedy motel lobbies. Over the glass dark
the Buick almost flies, ticking a song that sounds like liberty. The moon

backs into darkness, waning. You notice for the first time how much light
there is in darkness, everything shining—glint of quartz in the asphalt,

a sheerness in the canopy of trees, even the skin of passing motorists,
their faces grim or tired or singing, their teeth white, dazzling as wet

shells. Pale light of moss and mold, swamp water and alligator and every
slow-growing thing. You see light in the sunken ribs of a dead dog on

the sandy shoulder, still black husk in impeccable repose, facing
away from the road wind, slick casement of fur, smear of blood luminous

underneath. Everything you care for is awake. Your brother tosses, yeasty
warm in his trim cot, glow-in-the-dark stars stuck like wishes on the roof tiles.

You drive. Cut south, pass boiled peanut stands in the shadow of slick
new hospitals, slip under the false neon blue of floating Biloxi casino

barges, crossing yet another bridge to Ocean Springs. You do not, as the paper
will report, stop to pick up friends. You slip through the austere jade shimmer

of Gautier strip malls. You do not, as the paper will report, smoke or drink or
turn 360s on the lawn of First Baptist Church of Vancleave. All you do

is drive, pass the sandhill cranes of Pascagoula, shy in the marshes, prettier
than swans. For just one moment it is dark: pure black night. You

drive. And even though you see in the horizon's coming dawn a faint
splatter of blood, you turn around. Even though you see your father at

the table, shirtless, smoking Camels, you turn around. You hear
the echoing ring of the metal princess phone as it strikes your skull.   23

Your body, like a gift, soars through the night, toward his rage. Your brother,
dreaming, limbs perfect as new branches, sleeps, and so you turn around.

Head west now, toward home, all of it so fast, the oaks and the light and the
bridges and trees, until finally, you pull into the yard, kill the engine,

dust settling behind you in tufts like a ball of gauze thrown, unfurling in
the air, filthy and picturesque. The slider is lit up blue-white from the set,

the glass opaque and filmy in great swipes of dog nose and handprints in the
shape of waiting. You see your father: he's waiting at the table when you

slip in, set down the keys he picks up and slashes into your face. You take in
sharp breath and think: *night air*. The sun turns from pink to white, seeping into

every corner of the paneled room, you taste salt in your mouth and think: *rough
water on the Gulf*. And when the bone of your arm splinters like old kindling

stomped on in the yard, the sound is like a word whispered: *luck*.
When the phone cracks your skull you think:

freedom. You close your eyes and see darkness emerging
before you like a bridge. You're a breeze now, a shore

line, an engine ticking gently, night star, black dog, a bird
they can't see. You're a story in the paper: *No More Joy For Teen*.

You're fourteen, everything a possibility, nothing for sure.

II

Lumineux

SUNDAY BEST

Tell me again about the dream where we haul
the little girls out of the river and clothe them
in church dresses, smocked and ruffled, starched
stiff, buttoned up the back? The one where
each has her own bright cardigan, pearly
buttons dotted all the way up to the neck. I know
that (as church girls do) they all begin to wiggle
and fidget and pull at the elastic of their cotton
underthings. Remind me where it is they find
their dazzling daybreak-dove patent leather
Mary Janes and buckle up? Were the big
cranes there, or did we have to
heave the darling
cadavers up and out
ourselves? Did we drag them, or carry
them one by one, together? Did we lay them
to dry on the gilded levee grass? How did
we know they'd revive? All I remember is
this: girls marching down the levee, singing.

If he calls me, I will answer, if he calls me,
I will answer, if he calls me, I will answer, I'll be
somewhere a'workin' for my Lord.

Singing their puny sodden hearts out
into the horizon until they must eventually
hit town. We'll fetch the preacher
before he has his chance with them
again. There's time now
for us to rest here, in our sovereignty
of stillness. But you, suddenly then, down
from the bank and on your back on the shabby

silver dock, nude. Trucks flash by. No one
stops, no one looks, when I dip, platinum hair
loose, to lick from your skin the bloody
river water: it fills my lungs with a terrible
strangling torrent of arrogance.

Rescue: nothing but a myth
in crimson crinoline and
fancy cotton panties.

THREE MINUTES

What they do not tell you, when they bring you into the small room to counsel
you for ten minutes, asking *What brought you to your decision* and *Can you*

tell me how you feel? is that it will be painful like you could not imagine if you
have never had a man reach his fingers and then fist and then entire arm

up into you and suddenly open wide his hand. They do not tell you it will
hurt. What they say is, *cramping*. And when they take you into the room (the table

and stirrups, the machine that looks like a carpet steam cleaner) and tell you
to get undressed and put your underwear on top in the basket still littered with

pink lint, they do not tell you that later a girl with a pierced nose and pretty
eyes will inch the underwear up your legs and that there will be an enormous

sanitary pad inside them and she will leave them at your hips like a new
lover, too embarrassed to pull them farther down. She will leave them there

like that where she could reach her hand in freely and insert her slender
finger between your one pink lip and one brown lip, if she were to lie down

next to you and kiss you. They do not share that you will wish she would lie down
next to you and kiss you, that you will want her to cry with you about what she

watched inch in spasms down a thick plastic tube into a silver canister like
toxic waste on the way to a place it could never hurt anyone, never get

in their water or under their skin, where it could never create a permanent
stain on your brokedown heart etched: *rape*. What they do not tell you

is that the suction will not be even—what they say is *slight pulling* but
it will not be a slight pulling you feel over the din of the machine

which sounds not like *a dentist's tool* but like a rakish wail.
It will be a very distinct pulling and the part that I cannot imagine

them not telling you is that it will not be steady, it will be convulsing, like
someone very large breathing in and out of you. You will wish to be

raped over and over every day for the rest of your life rather than to feel it.
You've survived that this time, and all the other times as a child.

You will think you should have stopped it at the rape that brought you
here, should have never let the man in, so many years after the fights, the

scars, the jail time. You hoped for new beginnings. This wasn't the prom.
You're not straight. When he called, you laughed, sang a whole conversation

that sounded like let bygones be bygone—but how fast you hopped in
the shower, how dark you painted your lips. You fought him, hard,

and he laughed. He held your hair so tight. And when it happened it
was like that moment, after days of the tingling end of your tongue

trying to remember, that you do remember the name of the girl who
sat next to you in the first grade, the one who went missing but they

only looked for her in fields and forests and in the beds of rivers that
crossed your city, meeting out of town like a wishbone. It was over

and you knew it: pregnant. Like the killed girl found on the river
bottom, her body cold and loose and liquid, dredged up

with metal claws that clutched into the gingham sky-blue of
her dress. The *should have's* started then—left it at the phone call, met

somewhere for lunch, skipped the lipstick, fought harder, called the police, carried
to term, picked a name. You should have known you would look at your child

and see: your child. They do not mention this. This is up to you. But you
don't know in time. In the recovery room you will whisper over and over

I'm sorry

until you sleep, until they wake you, until they need the bed. It's your
decision, your right. They tell you that. But when you go home your

blood will drip for days on end into the toilet bowl, blossoming
an exquisite red-black like faith or futility.

For nothing.

They do not tell you this: that you will never be the same.

TO THE WOLVES

For Violet, Magnolia (died March 16, 2004)

How you must have suffered getting accustomed to
the void—alone in the soothing silk pod of my womb.
Violet, Magnolia. Violet, Magnolia. I loved to say it.
Not alone entirely, but alone. I wonder did your ears

notice the telltale cadence of only one underwater heart
beating? Could you, with your tiny legs and fingers, which
you liked to put into your mouth, feel the still ribs and skull
full of your sister's body? You were always the strong one.

They say that's true of all twins—there is always the one
who is slightly sturdier, slightly bigger, inching ahead in the
race to birth's finish line. You might have assumed, balanced
as you were in that bubble of loss and life, that something

terrible was wrong. You were to be my fourth born, surely
Magnolia—your silent twin—would have been fifth. How many
years I'd suffered, the flare of Lupus catching in my body
like a grass fire, wreaking havoc on my entire being.

Elbows, knees, fingers, even the tiny joints of my toes
scabbed over with that terrible, purple-red rash, turning
to brown, the mark of the ravaged wolf appearing on
my face. With each flare up I'd become almost elderly

in my gait and pace, until the rashes scabbed over
hard, turned dark hard russet, fell off. It was then, at the end
of that flare up, when I went to hear your heartbeats. I heard
yours, but your twin was already gone. Still I wanted you

something fierce. More, now. I worried and fretted and
tortured myself into the ground with every metaphor
on earth for the word *decay*. I have three
healthy babies (two still in diapers) I'd tell myself, peering
into the mirror. For weeks my face stayed clear. Every morning
I'd rise, look, say to my reflection *I have three healthy babies*
as if it were some sort of guarantee. I was, after all, the
world's most annoying pregnant person—no hint of

morning sickness, ankles lean as fine birch branches, hair twice
as thick and shining like sunlight, not a stretch mark in sight.
I prepared your room—took out the second crib and
brought in a big green leather rocking chair, imagined sitting

there, nursing you, looking out on the hundred yards of bayou
emptying into salty, wide open gulf, the waters merging,
the creatures staying mainly to one side, the other.
I have three healthy babies, I said again, not realizing

my husband stood in the closet not three feet away.
From behind the door: *Get over it*. And so I did, decided
to block your twin from my mind, shove her memory
away like so many fallen Magnolia trees, lost in piles

of roadside debris. I gained weight. My father died.
I finished your lilac nursery. I bought a set of old glass
and steel doctor's shelves and filled them with
treasures: a stuffed dog, perfect pinecone, a row

of your grandparent's bronzed baby shoes, a small
collection of heart-shaped rocks. My father sent you
an antique doll, with a porcelain face painted
all innocence, and a fine lace gown to cover

the rest of her. I waited. I mourned. I slept well.
March thirty-first I began to bleed. My husband
came home from his shift at the hospital
and found me on the silver-blue bedroom divan,

crying,
holding my belly.
What's wrong?
Blood.

He called a colleague from the other room, came back, said
We'll go over tomorrow first thing. Sleepless the whole night,
bleeding: he snored. Crossing west on the Biloxi Bridge by dawn:
I already knew. There was not just one dead baby, now there

were two. Magnolia, and you. It was too late for surgery—they
thought it best to induce. As I felt your big head
crowning, the doctor said, *Oh, she's blonde just like you,*
honey, and we smiled at one another. My husband cussed

under his breath, left the room. I held you both a while.
Violet, Magnolia. You were three times as big as Magnolia, she
looked something awful, her face by now deformed, her skin
the color of ruin. The next day, I sat in the pale purple nursery

at home and told my sweet three that you had
gone to God with Papa. They kept saying *APRIL FOOLS!*
APRIL FOOLS! and *APRIL FOOLS!* as if the news was
some kind of trick, until they noticed their mama's tears.

The oldest whispered *She's an angel now* in her girly pouty
baby voice. The next morning, as we were sitting at the formal
dining table for breakfast, all of us dressed finer than the nines
as usual, as if nothing had happened, we heard him call

to the kids from the back veranda. *Look kids! See?*
In his hands he held a minuscule baby hummingbird, dead.
He said, *Look at the violet of her throat and her dark*
dark eyes, doesn't she look sad? The kids, in habit, nodded

and recoiled. *This is like what Mama did to Violet.*
I gathered them to me, scurried them off to the shady
National Seashore behind our house. Walking through
the woods, in a hushed row behind me, the kids were nearly

soundless. Their footsteps fell like the steps of wolves. I felt
the familiar burn rise up in me, felt my joints scabbing
over, the mask of the wolf appearing on my face. A fox
crossed our path, the broken-wing distraction call

of killdeer filled the canopy of savannah pine, singing
Kill-dee-dee Kill-dee-dee Kill-dee-dee a frenzied lullaby.
As we passed the flat muddy bayou bank, a young
alligator didn't bother to flinch and neither did we.

At the end of the trail, we found our way to the wall
of the bridge, threw aside shoes, dipped in our feet.
The bayou passed beneath us into open Gulf, the sun
went down. In the profound haze of dusk, we didn't

even see the bottlefish floating in the tidal marsh, didn't
notice the fully-inflated blue-violet sail skimming
the surface, didn't suspect the mass of jellyfish-like
tangles underneath. Bottlefish are not jellyfish: they are

a entire damn colony, four kinds of minute, highly
modified subterranean souls, each needing the other
to survive. That bottlefish stung my girl something
fierce, leaving whip-like red welts on her alabaster leg.

The four of us made time, then, and I carried her, howling in pain, toward the light of our kitchen window, the bottle of vinegar waiting, back up the dark woodsy Nature's Way Trail, home; my two small boys following close behind.

HUSH

The summer you stop speaking is a wet one, rain
        pouring down, fat drops
of condensation dancing down your mother's
        ever-melting glass

of gin and Fresca. The air, heavy enough to hold
        in your palm, reeks of dank
moss and drowned potato bugs. As soon as you stop
        speaking, your world

becomes earsplitting—faucet handles screech in the cold
        porcelain sink, water roaring
in the walls through copper pipes, baseboards scraped
        bare by so many

wood roaches and mice, the one fallen column
        of the porch, hollow, where
a raised whisper, the hiss of your parents' secret
        exchange, threatens

the brittle balance of it all. They don't notice your silence
        for days, but
he knows. After dinner he slices into a square icebox
        cake, pauses, staring as if

at the double rectangles of turned earth still fresh in the far
        corner of the yard. You simply
stop talking, and it's easy. You do the things
        you're told, make your bed first

thing, take your dish to the sink, comb your hair, part
              straight, and fasten bows on each side.
Your father stops talking too, but only to you. No one
              notices. Each time you slip out

from the hall bathroom he's there waiting, a smile
              and a swift, sharp smack
across your bottom hard enough to let you know
              who's boss. You know. You slip

outside, hopping along the toad-dotted walkway. You take off
              on your brother's bike, standing
on the pedals to reach the high handlebars, riding like
              that, like a tottering lopsided

old lady, pumping up the lane. At the top of
              the hill, where bayou turns to
piney woods, you spot them. The French sisters—Candy
              and Cookie—twins,

whose house is a replica of your own, upended and facing
              north, but otherwise
identical. You've been coming here every day for a week—
              the French family van

backing into the neighborhood the best thing to happen
              all summer—you are wretched jealous
of their beauty, bandana halters knotted over baggy
              men's dress slacks (from when

their daddy worked for the man, cut off just below
              the knee, belted and tied with
ropes and braids and beads. When they whip
              their matching waist-length hair

out of their eyes, their faces are a dotted snowy
        hillside, berries fallen in the freeze.
And their hands, moving as quickly as they do
        between one another, are long and

the beds of their nails are pale and graceful. You know
        the ASL alphabet from school, but that's
all. Your questions arrive as quickly as a tick getting off
        of a dog. The picnic table

is covered with sturdy string and big wooden beads
        painted orange and red and
green, by pine needles fallen in bunches from the canopy
        of woods, by scissors and soda cans

and bottles of polish. They teach you to sign: a few words
        a day. The first:
braid, sky, sun, knees. The second: *tree, sister, table,*
        kiss. You sit in the corrugated

sunlight while their hands fly between knots
        and conversation, and they laugh
their far away laugh that sounds like a girl
        locked in a metal shed, trying

to get out. You hum a tune your
        father used to sing
when you were small. On Wednesdays you
        finish the belt. The circles

under your eyes are the exact green of moss growing
        thick on cold boulders
of bayou banks. That day they show you: *pinch, love, drink*
        and (when their daddy appears with more

Mellow Yellows) *father*. He seems nice, Mr. French.
    You tie the knots of your belt
too tight and try not to think of the night
        before.

Mr. French gives you a thumbs-up, as if you're the
        winner of a beauty contest wearing
his cut off polyester orange plaid leisure slacks.
        Mr. French has a habit of throwing out

his arms to the whole earth and signing, *This is
        the life!*
You wonder about your own father, how long he'd been
        planning his move.

Perhaps he thought it up the day we came home
        from vacation
at Auntie Lina and Uncle Lou's soy and strawberry
        farm, only to find our two

poodles dead on the back porch, shriveled and
        thin and rained on and
reeking. Miss Oineida always kept the dogs
        when we traveled, spoiled

them bad, but this time she passed away the day
        we left and her family came
from Tupelo, held a wake and funeral, had a big
        reception laid out nice

in the rear yard. No one knew about the dogs. The first
        night home you and mama
put the dogs in boxes, wrapped up in Easter paper
        covered in pastel

crosses, and burried them in the back corner
            of the yard, as deep as you, leveling
the soil. Maybe it was then. You smooth the bumpy
            length of your new belt

and wonder. Or maybe it was the night you
            first figured a way to keep him
out, wedging the tall desk chair so tight
            under the knob. That night, waiting

as you did, you saw the knob rattle, then
            quiet. The next day your chair
was in the kindling pile. That night you
            came up with a better plan; you ask him

and mama to tuck you in, you say
            your prayers right
nice and close your eyes, faking
            happy slumber. The instant

they leave the room, you
            slide open the window, pop
the screen, hop out and are gone. You sit on
            the two fresh graves and wait.

He comes, wanders the corners
            of your room, sees the open
window, places a hand through it carefully as if
            the glass might still be there.

You raise your arms and sign *This is the...* but
            he spots your blue floral gown
in the moonlit yard and shuts the window, pulls
            the latch. For three nights

after that you sleep, in your own room, in your
   own bed, with the door
open, peacefully, no interruptions.
   Your father, as he passes

on the way to bed, is singing lightly
   You are my sunshine, my only
sunshine, you make me happy when skies are
   gray. You'll never know, dear,

how much I love you, please don't take my sunshine
   away.
You get up early every day and put on Mr. French's
   pants and stand-ride

the 5-speed up to see the twins. The day it
   happens you coast down
the hill home and commit to memory the signs for
   pretty and *love* and *secret.*

You are sound asleep in bed, dreaming
   of the bayou, only silence
and a pair of red-headed
   woodpeckers to share

your picnic. In the dream there is
   a panic of wings, of woodchips
falling, of air too heavy for flight.
   You're pinned.

41

You wake, see him hovering, your
   door shut tight,
nightgown and covers thrown
   to the floor, skin

clammy, cold. The room
        is filled with night air, the scent
of locust husks, of pine pollen and rock moss
        and road dust and frogs. As he

lifts you into his arms: you don't
        hear, you don't make
a sound. Out the window, into
        the yard, plodding slowly

he carries you to the back behind
        the pine grove.
You see in the cerulean moonlight a new
        grave, a larger, longer one,

wormy and fresh, closer to the fence. Fireflies dart
        in the trees above
and suddenly you, too, are flying, fast, through
        darkness. You

hit bottom, hard. It takes your breath like
        falling straight backwards
off a swing. You can't think of anything but
        the playground

as great clods of dirt sift down on your stomach
        and hips, your
naked chest, filling the white hollow at
        the base of your neck.

42

The dirt comes in heaves, topping you head
        to toe and even though
it stings, you keep your eyes open, silent
        prayer begging

God to let you fly away. You see his white
              cotton boxers shining bright; his glasses
like flashes of moonlight. Shoveling, he turns
              away from you and swings back to the grave.

Those glasses like warning lights at the edge
              of a track, where there
aren't any safety bars. The dirt piles up
              and suddenly you hear it,

your whole world—locusts and crickets,
              hanging moss shifting
in the oak, zipping wing of firefly, a hound
              howling in a far off yard.

You hear the music of your world and it sounds
              so far
away, a twangy echo kept in a plastic
              coffee can.

And that's when you hear it, your father's
              voice, the same words
whispered, sung quiet and sincere,
              You'll never know

dear, how much I love you. Please don't take
              my sunshine away.
He grabs you up and out and holds you
              in his lap and

cries, muddying your tummy. *If you*
              leave me, to love
another, you'll regret it all of
              your days.

He holds you, rocks the dawn in, and you
      hum the song with
him and cling like the saved
      do, and vow

to stop speaking, in the hush of that night.

LUMINEUX

On forgiving my father before his death

It's like silence, the black sky full of stars like silver
jacks and a pale blue rubber ball moon. Like sitting

at the breakfast table, the windows sending sheer
envelope-shaped shards of silky white light across

the lawn, right before you pick up the phone to call.
Like the moment you first hear his voice—after the nine

years—and remember at once all the good about
him, right before he says, *Hello?* Like evening, children

circling in the yard—white pajamas, hyacinth-scented
hair—the moment you see the bug on the baby, right

before you slap, spill blood. Like laughter. New pencils.
Like a pink paper permission slip, your foot resting on

the first metal step of the yellow bus. Like reading that
story in the paper, three boys drowning in the bayou,

standing later over the bodies of your own boys, asleep,
watching their lanky sets of ribs rise and fall and rise

and fall again. Like breathing. Like night air, right
before it rains. Like morning, just before you've opened

your eyes. Like the moment you cross the bridge
of dreams and realize that the kisses grazing your

skin like bayou light are from your lover, right before
you turn to her and smile. It's like that day, driving home

across the bayou bridge, when it starts to rain in bright
sunlight, and your daughter says, *Look Mama, it's*

sparkling! Like the bayou—the subterranean
darkness of the water punctuated with trees. Like

stripping off all your clothes in the crisp air, the moment
you dive into the bayou, the water bitter, thick

with silt and little specks of gold, right before
you surface and breath another time. Like the evening

your lover appears with a strand of flawless, dark-as-night
pearls, right before you turn, lift your hair and feel the clasp

against your neck. Like singing loud as you can
the tune of *The Yellow Rose of Texas,* speeding

with the top down and the salty Gulf glittering
silver, sugar-white sand for miles,

I heard a Fly buzz— when I died—
The Stillness in the Room

Was like the Stillness in the Air—
Between the Heaves of Storm—

Like finding in the red velvet abyss
of your jewel box the old photo of yourself

in pink tights and tiara, chest bare, four
years old, sound asleep with your father

on the nubby brown rec room couch, his arm thrown
over your tiny waist, his dreaming filled with bliss, right

before you turn the photo over to see your
mother has penciled just one word: *happiness*.

TRASH LADY

Night sliced open with
wind-driven rain
in sheets, stars
unseen. She wakes
to the sound of her
leaning on the truck's
dark horn, to the noxious
scent of rubbish smudging
through the screens.
She rises, runs (white
gown, feet bare, hair
wild, rain affixing silk
to skin, an animate
shimmering predawn
papier-mâché) and leaps
into the cab. Curb to
curb the cans rise up
and tip life altogether—mango
peel, shit in bags, a sapphire
stud, soggy condoms, crayoned
papers, rancid rib roast—in.
Shattering bottles, crushed
pastille, nibbled slipper, letters
like frantic birds:
everything lovely falls.
She sleeps: that ripe
lap enough for
her rotting heart, her
tinfoil wings enough
for their
freedom.

III

The Love Brigade

VIDALIA

There's a drop-out girl on my block
now (eleven going on seventeen) who
each day sits on Sweet Earl's front porch

eating a purple onion like it's a black
plum, luscious and ripe. A stippled
beauty—rail thin, endless limbs, jade

eyes, snarled copper hair to the
waist, greasy Levi's, a chopped,
mini-length old wedding gown.

She takes the day entire
to eat that onion, last bite beckoning
night. She's stuck a galaxy of

shoplifted glow-in-the-dark
stars on the falling-panel
ceiling in their bedroom.

All night Sweet Earl kisses her
violet prize, and bites her
there—hard.

Even then, sultry blood
rising, she still don't
shed a tear.

DISGRACE ARIA

I'm five years old, I'm
sexy. I got
strong little muscles. I got
long little legs. I'm nimble, I can
do the Chinese splits. I do
ballet three whole hours a day.
I bind my feet in pale pink
satin shoes and at night
I suck the blood from
my sore toes. When my
mama comes in and catches me
she goes, *Shame*
on you.
Shame on you.

★

I'm five years old. I am
sexy. I like to hang out in
the garage. We've got a big
bumper pool table and I'm
the best girl on the block.
I can fit an entire shiny black
8-ball into the small pink cavern of my
mouth—I can't close my teeth
on it or anything, but I don't
gag. And the boys on the block
pay me money to do it and when they
laugh
my heart goes,
Shame on you. Shame, shame, shame
on you.

★

I'm five years old—I'm sexy.
I like to watch public TV
in the afternoons. I like ZOOM
and Electric Company.
Shhhhhhhhh-ot.
SHOT!
Sssssssssss-ilk.
SILK!

I like to put on mama's black
nightie with no undies. And when
I sit on the hardwood floor it's cold
against my skin and I pull my
feet up behind my head and I *spin!*
And daddy's 'cross the room with his
vodka on the rocks and even though
he's smiling, even though he's
watching and the scar that snakes his
throat is turning blue, he goes, *Shame*
on you. Nasty! Shame on you.

★

I'm five years old. Sexy.
I don't have very many friends.
I go to the park Sundays with my
brother: he doesn't have
very many friends. We play
stickball with a stick I find and
a ball he brings in the pocket of his
jeans. He throws, I hit. I can't
throw. And when he goes to pee

against the haunted weeping willow
I run up behind him and grab his
little pecker and I *laugh!* I think
it's so funny when I do that, I feel
so funny when I do that
but he just puts it away
real fast and he goes,
Shame on you.
God damn.

★

I'm five years old. I'm sexy.
I can take it down the throat
so much easier since the surgery.
The Dr., he goes, *The mass at the back*
of her throat is harmless to mama.
I knew what it was all along—a pink
scar of courage, not
stupid cancer.
My daddy, he had
cancer and he
didn't have to do
anything
at all to get it.
I
worked.
I'm
proud.
I don't
gag. And when daddy
comes in and one night I'm
waiting, I got
no clothes on, I got my lips

painted red, I got my pointe shoes
laced up super tight. I'm in the middle
of the moonlight on my toes and I go
C'mon Daddy, c'mon, Now
you ready to do me right?
And I guess I'm getting
too old or maybe I'm
not sexy 'cause he just
turns red and
turns around and
marches out the door.
When he's walking down the hall
to his and mama's room I don't even
care that it's fully way past dark
and everyone is sleeping. I'm there
and I'm naked in the moonlight on my
toes, alone, and I go, you
know, I practically
scream it, it feels so
funny when I
do it
but I do it, I just
say it, I go,
Shame. On. You.

Shame.

On.

You.

LITTLE VIOLENCE

A woman like that is not ashamed to die.
I have been her kind.
—Anne Sexton, 'Her Kind'

I feel her there, behind my ribs where they hit the bus stop pole
after the back wheel of the motorbike tilted up

in response to the front wheel bucking against the curb,

hurtling me, a fierce ballerina in pink and black, through
the air. My little violence is right there, where my ribs

cracked, puncturing each lung. She can't catch her breath.

Come out, little violence, come to me like you did
then, after the surgery, waving your bare arms

at visitors going by. Sutures, drains, scabs: all

a lazy pastime, an exhibition of the expanse between
blood and pride. Little violence, you would not abide

the healing. Oh, sweet, diamond-crusted pumpkin

of brutality, bring me a girl who'll slap me during sex without
asking first. Bring me a pretty pocketbook full of

folding money on which someone has scrawled, in black

indelible ink, radif-less ghazals, and filled in the numbered
corners with girlish stars and hearts. Slide into my lap

and fill my white lace tap pants full of moonlight the blue

of bleak horizons and nevermore. Stand up on my thighs, that's
right, you can reach, breath tender stepladders of smarting

raised welts into my mouth. Let me wake singing with pain

and love you at once. Let me scrawl your name along all
my taut scars—*dearest one, babydoll, beloved sprite*

of cruelty. Let me run my fingers through your silver reeds

of sorrow then fix my chignon into a scarlet moment of
despair. Peel the tangerines with your tapered pale fingers

and drop the oil-fragrant curls onto the rug (I'll throw myself

on the bed.) Let my lover's other lover call ten times
for every orgasm: let her frustration keep pace

with my oblivion. I'm getting to like you now,

my little hidden destruction, waiting as you are like an old
black rotary phone on the mirrored table in the front

hall of my heart. Leave my longing for you, naked, all

atremble. And when finally you do come, let me
refuse you. Hold my ankles tight, tear all the clean

white bandages away, bite, scream, stamp your

nude feet. I'll still leave, dragging your needs
behind me like a disgrace train on my dress as I go.

KEEPSAKE SERENADE

Let me remember only the starry explosion

                of our limbed violence. Let me see

the faint reflection on my thighs, through

           the windowpane of stockings, the blue-green

bruise of your bite. Let me wear the sweater

             you bought to match those marks

day after day until

                  it falls to ruin. Let me fall

one more time into our night

            before I set it away, like a skein of scarlet

silk ribbon, thrown and unfurling

                 into the battered sky.

Let me call myself: *Girl.*

             Your voice is silence. Your voice

is the color of birds in mean flocks

            over the fields: a fast shadow, passing.

Let me catch the ribbons falling from the sky

and bind my wrists and ankles tight. Erase

this freedom: keep me bound in ecstasy.

Constrain me in sorrow's flaxen

destruction. Let me have courage enough

for your absence. Let me adore

everything: every golden corner of your

quiet soul, every splintered moment of your

ravenous heart; let me take the palm prints

from your gut and devour

their slap-shaped wounds like so much

memory candy. Let me give you midnight-colored

velvet pouches filled with searing inverse oil lanterns

to cast darkness on your every regret. Let me

adore you. Every splintered shard

of your furious, exquisite heart.

Let me, please.

I'm soon to forget.

CITY OF MOONLIGHT

I should have known the first night I met you
it would not end well. I chose to meet in the
Japanese garden in the womb of the biggest
park in Sacramento, which is the only city
in which I will love you. I don't yet know
that you won't travel, that an airplane feels
like a death machine waiting to gobble
you up. Travel for you is a lake
one hour away. We dive in naked, slick
as seals. No matter how deep I dive, hoping
to find a portal to the other side
of the Earth, I keep hitting
the drowned metal bottom of
our ruin. I don't know yet, the night
in the garden, that death
is your constant seduction. That
death knocks at the slammed
hood of your heart, over the
engine of every part of life
at which you throw yourself.
These are the moments you
want to die: when you quit
that job, when your mother
sent the girly birthday card, when
your blonde ex took up with
your friend, when you remember
shirtless days as a child where you
climbed trees and ran in the woods and
didn't know yet what gender was, when
the medicine is changed, when the day
is too quiet, when the night comes.

When the night comes you want
to die. Sometimes I try to lift you
out of darkness and sometimes
I want to crawl inside your darkness
and sharpen my teeth which
I will later use to bite your flesh
to remind you you're alive. I see
the deepest pain when you recall
the last girl, and the one before
that. The way you throw yourself
on the guilt of it all like a funeral
pyre, burning in the flames of
your own seduction dance. I wonder
if your blondes are
interchangeable, if I am just
another water queen to put out
your terrible fire. We're all
your blondes, spinning delicate
webs in the galaxy of your
soul and pissing golden lava on
the webs until everything you are
is caught up and sticky and the
only way out is death. I don't want
you to die, so I keep spinning, keep
pissing, keep holding my breath
and diving deeper. I don't know
anything at all about why I
love you. Except for your haunted
eyes and long fingers and fried
chicken addiction and the way you
hold my hair all in a bunch at the back
of my head and enjoy almost
letting me kiss you. All I know is
this: that I brought you to the cacti

garden. That I find you in
the city of moonlight and the air
is heavy with the stardust
of my desire. That your past
is a junkyard full of rust and
glory. That you are made of shattered
glass in river bottoms, of fallen stars
in truck beds, of all I forgot I knew
until I met you. That some nights
will break us, and some nights will
put us back together, but
they will both end in moonlight.
That you are beautiful like
moonlight, like stardust, like midnight
tears and comets. In this part
of the story stars sway
like celebration balloons
of another day allowed us
on this earth. That suffering
is an embossed ticket, letters
raised like slapped skin, to
transformation, incandescent
and earned. That the first time
I see you I think, *There, that one, they*
write my name in blood on the scorched earth
of possibility. I know that you are
terribly late but the crappy pink
peony and your cowboy shirt
are a midsummer Valentine. Because

I want to believe. I want to believe that
the dark shoreline of my heart
has a portal, and that you, with your
cocky-ass walk and your
eyes the color of silver caskets, can

stroll through that portal and buy me
candy bars and mother of pearl
anchors to weigh down the horrible
floating away I always feel
from this world. All I know is that
you and the stars are the
same thing: made of dust and
wonder. All I know, as you breathe
fables through your tongue into
my ear for hours in the
dark, cacti rising up behind you
like a city of pain, is that
you tell me such terrible
stories and to me they
sound like home.

THE LOVE BRIGADE

I tried to get you to kill me. You skirted
the edge of male and female, you said, *two
spirit*. That wasn't all. I knew within you
was a man of fury and a broken
boy with legs made of sticks and
mud and a sullen teen who
hid his wild desire with
shyness and Oklahoma
swagger. Every time I
kissed you I summoned
them. The souls you contain
are the shadow's echo between
the endless fence and the long field where you
throw me down. Down in the dirt, between
the cabbages blooming like wild
vaginas, green and the size of your
lips when I close my eyes, taste
your jagged-glass sex with my
tongue. You threw me down, down
to the place where I was the small
girl in a thin bed, sky blue
panties wrapped around my
ankles like a shackle. We met
wound to wound. We are
lost, together at once, in our
dissociation. This
is the dirty part of dissociation and
we have confessed that
we love it. My scraped sex fucks
your two-by-four behind
the barn, beating us back

to something like the beginning
of who we were
before. Who we were before
it all, before the slapped hand
on the ass, the gathered, strangled
wrists above the head, that one
imaginary day in our mirrored/respective
childhoods when we were
untouched. We don't know what it
means to feel clean. We are welted skin
smeared with memory and
forgetting-mud, we are behind
the closed door, we are the endless
night, the two hours when mama
goes to town, we are the come around
to wanting it, we are the pact
we made with the ones that fucked
the baby-good out of us. In the dirt I
whisper all your names in your
seashell-shaped ear. I know them
by heart. I don't care which one
of you I'm fucking now, I'm fucking
all of you, the white
suit, the captured soldier, the baby black
bear with sharp claws that paw
my nipples (suck, suck, suck, suck, mama).
I'm fucking all of you because I
know you. We tell each other our
secrets but we don't say them
in the world because there is a dirty
string in the dirt yard that stepping over
means we wanted it. We were trained up
good like tiny sex soldiers, indoctrinated
into the ecstacy of shame. This is what we

learned, and it still feels good. And every time
I come I both love you and I hate
myself. Everything I forgive in you
turns on me in the end—bad
girl, naughty, dirty, filthy spit-shined
shame. Maybe you're teaching me
how my desire is a new way to make
1000 nights of childhood
right. Maybe you're fucking my
suicide-bone, my sex-knife plunged
into all the fleshy places you aren't
supposed to feel desire. Where
are we? In the dirt field the canopy
bed the birds nest loft of your
place. Loft is just another word for
ghosts, which cling to the steep stairs
up to your bed. All the white shirts
once made here hang like
so many funeral parade signs.
All we make here is
sex, is fucking, is the intersection of
our wounds and our wanting.
I ask you to hit me.
You beg me for
a safe word. I tell you nothing
is safe, a safe word means
a way out and I look at you
close up as I lick the
corner of your mouth and

know that we were never
safe and never
will be. You're dirty
like me. You're fractured
like me. You're a dozen

different pieces of the same
girl-shaped boy. You're the
razor blades on my thigh
at fifteen. You're the
fingerprint bruises on my
four-year-old chest. You're
the moment before
the moment
that it all
makes sense.

IV

Paper Sack of Majesty

WISHBONE

You are made
of undiscovered truth. Nothing
is new: everything

is fixed. Fixed in time, fixed
in the shaded
corner of your restless soul.

You ball up
fury and toss it into a field of
tall grasses.

Your hands are strong and made
for my tongue,
the jagged roof of my mouth.

Your hands
are deliverance. You rip up
history, soak it

in Malbec, pour it at the base
of nevermore.
You take my every piercing ache

and wrap it
in linen, tie a fine bow, wait
for the catastrophic

wake of my eternal ravenous lust
to hit, salt water
in your eyes, nothing calm, before

you pull
the ribbon loose, bite apart
the knot.

You are made of the moment before
the moment
the sky turns black. Tell me your dark

heart bursts
with my mercurial nectar. Tell me
the day

for you holds the ruins of
sunlight and
fast tongues and fabric rough and

lovely, falling.
Hold me aloft while we construct
debauchery.

Tell me trust is an etched white bone
dissecting
the heart. Carved into one side,

You cannot
escape this good fortune.
And into the other,

We will never get tired
of this.
Take hold of the bone, close

your eyes, think of
our kingdom of nothingness, when
all that is

is our delicate furious
devotion, make a fine
wish. Now, pull.

PAPER SACK OF MAJESTY

You change one stone to diamond
and think: that's enough. What if

I take your handful of stones, devour
them one by one, restore them in my gut

to ferocious rapture, pouring from my
luminous fingertips a torrential onslaught

of compassion? What if my radiant fingers
pierce your windswept skin, extract

the terrible, outraged abundance? What if
I take that pulpy wrath, hurl it onto

the bedroom wall? Now, it's art.

Drink the last drop of yesterday's
violence wine. Fall naked to the sheets,

hung over one last time with misery's
eternity-pact. Wait. I'm coming in my torn

black lace, with everything you dread
wrapped tight, in my paper sack of majesty.

MAP

Her perfume like fallen
dark cherries, smashed on
Salvation Road, a two way
on the levee, with the
convent behind, high
above the sinister gun
-metal gray of the river.
Seared on your neck, her
burnt-sugar kiss
a salivated map
of every past moment that
arrived unpardoned—brutal
turn into another empty
room, cutting
velvet rucksacks
to store all your confidential
rapture.

Keep driving.

Ten and two.

Eyes on the road.

She's got a mouth full
of razor-sharp scarlet
pits, but a heart
crowded with
rose-cut dazzling
desire.

THE SEASON OF ORDINARY TIME

In memory of Elizabeth and Abraham Duman

> *God did not make death, nor does he rejoice*
> *in the destruction of the living. For he fashioned all things*
> *that they might have being; for justice is undying.*
> —Catholic Nun's Liturgy of the Hours,
> Wisdom 1:13-14a. 15, (Office for the Dead)

This is how it happens. It is a Thursday, an ordinary day. Eli is in his
room, perhaps, making sense of the intricate configuration of Legos for

Johannes, because everybody knows a three-year-old can't make
a spaceship that can speed all the way to the stars. It says on the box,

even, *six and up*. Johannes stands watching. Mama is in the kitchen,
cleaning up crusts from the four big kids' lunches, the kids who marched

down the steep grade of Scenic Hills Drive in Clarkston, Washington, to
school. Only the little ones, the last four, are home. Only Eli and Johannes,

only Abraham, who sucks his thumb and resists his nap on the little towel
by the back kitchen door. Abraham, who likes to pretend he is a puppy

and so sleeps on his towel, in a public room, curled up, eventually twitching
in dreams. Only tiny Ruby Rose, napping in her hand-me-down crib,

battered with stickers and the wear of biters, smelling like the sugar-cookie
ten-year-oblivion-of-lullabies-sung-and-milk-sucked and babies eased

off Mama's breast into the velvety sheets. Daddy has just now left.
For that one instant, after the kiss, after the front door shuts, after the

phone rings and goes unanswered, everything is quiet, the same, filled
with grace. And then Mama, who prays that God will destroy the veiled

chaos in her heart, goes down the hall. Goes walking so quietly, the same
way she walked down the marble hall of the convent so many years

before. Even then she had a secret, a love for a boy (bigger than her desire
for poverty, chastity, obedience). Even then, what she wanted was to be

pure and right and good. And she was. She was. She planted the flowers
and baked the casserole and glued the elbow macaroni on paper plates,

on Sunday mornings, into the shape of the cross—or a dove—and let the kids
go wild in the corner of the social hall with silver and gold gilded spray paint

because she believed that grace should come with some sort of
beauty, even the ragged, silly, messy beauty of children.

But on this morning, her poverty of heart leads her toward the safe, toward the
.44-caliber revolver. She believes with conviction and calm that this, now,

is her calling. She takes the .44 and goes back to the kitchen, where Abraham
finally sleeps his puppy sleep on the towel, hours before he expects his bowl

of lunch, which he eats like the good little puppy he is—no fork, no
spoon, on all fours, loudly. This is when Elizabeth gets out

the lined paper and sharpened yellow pencil. She knows enough
to write notes (*You're the oldest, you call for help*). She knows enough

to write notes (*Lord, open my lips and my mouth will proclaim
your praise*). She knows enough to write notes, the Liturgy

of the Hours coming back to her (*The bones that were crushed
leap for joy before the Lord*). And then she puts down

the pencil, picks up the .44, and shoots Abraham first, her sweet little
fuzzy cold-nosed beloved, in the back. And the blood spreads

around him like a new blanket, warm, filled with Mama's intention.
She holds the .44 close to her chest, both hands grasping it, as she

goes down the hall. And when she enters the baby's room, she
breaths in their grassy tart scent and thinks about the way that

Ruby Rose, even at two months, will horde a mouth of breast
milk, how she can only slip into dreams with that final mouthful

of blue-white nectar filling her cheeks, and so, she looks down
on her, and shoots her too. In the tummy. The baby's eyes

open, and a rivulet of still-warm milk comes streaming down
her barely still-furry cheek. Mama hears footsteps in the hall, and

turns, then. The boys are running. Now she's got to
work, the kingdom of Heaven knows no ease. Mama goes

into the hall after the boys, and she points the .44
at Johannes, and fires. A spaceship falls. The house is

quiet, and paucity of thought or perhaps the volume
of the ringing in her ears or perhaps

a kind of ragtag last minute grace, allows her
to forget Eli. Big Eli who won't go to first grade until

next year. She walks to the kitchen. She doesn't lie down
by her baby boy, twenty-one months of puppy perfection.

She doesn't write another note or clean up or make a call.
She simply points the .44 at her heart and fires. Four hours

later Daddy comes home. Mama is dead, Abraham is dead.
Johannes and Ruby Rose are shaking and bleeding. And he

makes a call. Sirens roar up Scenic Hills Drive, arrive as if
they simply appeared, a moment later, from space.

It is only after the men come rushing in, after
the gurneys unfold everywhere, that they realize

Eli is missing. They search. Under the beds, and in
the closets, in the pantry, and over the fence. There is

not a sound. They send out a call on the static-filled
radio. And then Daddy opens, by chance or grace

or wisdom, the battered hamper in the hall. And there
is Eli—who doesn't pop up like a terror-filled surprise, who

doesn't leap with relief into Daddy's arms—who lies, tucked
deep into the hamper, his mother's dirty nightie held tight

in one fist, the thumb of that hand shoved deep
in his mouth, sound asleep. Waiting. Sleeping

in the laundry, the smell of his whole family cradling him
in the very last hours of simple.

And he slept.

PROMENADE DE LA HONTE

That girl, she's wearing yesterday's pink-and-turquoise
dress, shoes gone missing, marching once again in her private

suprême procession. She's snapped on for the umpteenth time
the sequined feathered Mardi Gras mask, to hide the

black eye dark as a Quarter night. Her pockets
full of swamp grass and smashed Croquembouche, hair

a windstorm of sin, marching right by Old Ursuline Convent
while the academy girls double-dutch, swinging plaid skirts

in the golden Quarter light. As anybody knows, she lives
above the Cafe D'Or, up the azure tile steps around

back, her starched white garments trembling
on the balcony (half-festering with steam) always

betraying the way the door locks when she arrives, the
sound of her father's gin-soaked fury echoing

in the grand piano's bowels. She walks from one hard punch
in the face to another, because that's what

she has been raised to know, that's
what she has been raised to take, what she

has been trained to carry, the scent of it a dead
giveaway, that sweet bouquet of atonement and brioche.

THE WATERMARK

Three days after the storm

It is almost ten in the morning, and finally I've come
out of the alley, where I dole like contraband to the
residents of Red Cross Shelter #13, out of black plastic

garbage sacks the entire wardrobe of my three children

and myself. There is, in shelters such as these, a
No Acquisitions policy, so that the displaced cannot
waste too much space along the slick floors

with *unnecessary belongings*. But I've a house

twenty-seven blocks away, chock full of a terrible, lucky
abundance, untouched by storm surge, by the salty
seep of rising flood, untouched, even, by wind. Folks sift

through the stacks of clean underwear like shoppers

flipping through stacks of dusty albums at a Saturday
morning tag sale. With the clothes it's grab fast and
go, pulling them on over what they already have,

right there in the alley. But the eager girl from

Ann Arbor, with the telltale white tee—that bold Red
Cross emblazoned in the middle, ironed creases
at each sleeve—has looked twice out the window

on the alley, so I slam the hatch and go in. We don't need

another incident with an officer, like yesterday. I thought
Billy Gautier, who lost everything, has his whole family
camped out crammed in his station office, might strangle

the poor girl. The social hall is nearly untouched.

Yes, the walls are still wet, all the way up to almost
the top. The tiles of the floor lift in patterns, leaving
asbestos shadows on the undersides of mismatched

bedding strewn across the floor. Yes, the splintered

piano keys are wedged into windowsills and the back
wall is a papier-mâché mural with inches of the pulpy grayish
remains of a thousand hymnal pages. There is no longer

a door, now only a way. But the hall is still here. I stand

behind the counter of what used to be the kitchen,
passing out granola bars and bottles of water to
survivors—the families from the big houses

on East Beach who will rise up, carried away to family

in the Delta by tomorrow noon, latest. I hand over
apples to single men, wanderers come to Ocean Springs
from New Orleans with the season change, to the frantic

sunburned families from, as we all called them in town,

The Complexes—dingy apartment homes right
on the water—filled with the working poor, disabled,
elderly, welfare debutantes with hourly rates, crack

dealers, all "Coast Trash" living in the Savanna Luxury Estates.

They're easy to spot, the ones from the complexes, in
the shade-dappled rusty light from mud-crusted
windows, their feet bare, eyes hollow, as they slink up

to the front of the line, passing through the shadow

of the fallen church steeple out front, pointing
not up now to the heavens, but over, choked
with moss, like a shaggy exit sign pointing west,

commanding everyone *GET OUT*. They move

slowly, heads down, stringy hair thick with storm water
silt, wearing my dresses, my jeans, a tall man with a black eye
squeezed into my boy's sleeveless New Orleans Saints jersey,

his red belly jutting out between the borders of the jersey

and his rigid, mud-thick bell bottom jeans. And at the way
back tail of the line, there is a girl, a sort of ordinary girl, pretty
in a way you think a pattern of cheap duct tape stuck

to a wall after a makeshift sign has fallen is pretty, found

art, eyes black as midnight, freckles either God-given
skin starlight or simply splattered mud, in her fragile communion
dress edged in Irish lace, Social Security number still scrawled

in Sharpie on the alabaster underside of her arm

in her father's slanted hand. And on her dress: a
meridian, smack dab across the middle of her sunken
chest, right where her frenzied swimming heart nearly

drowned, but was baptized by fire instead, a spare but

graced rebirth. This almost lovely scrappy girl, possibility
in a ravaged dress, catastrophe spelled out in seed
beads and sequins, alive, above the watermark.

ACKNOWLEDGEMENTS

The author acknowledges the following journals, where versions of these poems first appeared:

New Letters ('Three Minutes'), *Plum Review* ('To the Wolves'), *Tupelo Quarterly* ('Vidalia,' 'Keepsake Serenade'), *Sarnac Review* ('Joy Ride'), *Cutthroat* ('The Water,' 'The Watermark,' 'The Quiet'), *The Best of Cutthroat* ('The Quiet'), and *ArtHotel* ('The Quiet').

THANKS

The author expresses gratitude to the following people and
organizations for support in the writing and making of this
book: Eyewear Publishing and Todd Swift, Kelly Davio, and
Edwin Smet; The Squaw Valley Community of Writers;
Lucille Clifton; The Napa Valley Writers' Conference;
Dennis Schmitz; Avery, Grayson, and Aidan Anderson;
The Haven Foundation and Stephen King; Elena Kalis;
and PEN America.

EYEWEAR PUBLISHING

EYEWEAR'S TITLES INCLUDE

EYEWEAR POETRY

KATE NOAKES CAPE TOWN
SIMON JARVIS EIGHTEEN POEMS
ELSPETH SMITH DANGEROUS CAKES
CALEB KLACES BOTTLED AIR
GEORGE ELLIOTT CLARKE ILLICIT SONNETS
HANS VAN DE WAARSENBURG THE PAST IS NEVER DEAD
BARBARA MARSH TO THE BONEYARD
MARIELA GRIFFOR THE PSYCHIATRIST
DON SHARE UNION
SHEILA HILLIER HOTEL MOONMILK
MARION MCCREADY TREE LANGUAGE
SJ FOWLER THE ROTTWEILER'S GUIDE TO THE DOG OWNER
AGNIESZKA STUDZINSKA WHAT THINGS ARE
JEMMA BORG THE ILLUMINATED WORLD
KEIRAN GODDARD FOR THE CHORUS
COLETTE SENSIER SKINLESS
ANDREW SHIELDS THOMAS HARDY LISTENS TO LOUIS ARMSTRONG
JAN OWEN THE OFFHAND ANGEL
A.K. BLAKEMORE HUMBERT SUMMER
SEAN SINGER HONEY & SMOKE
RUTH STACEY QUEEN, JEWEL, MISTRESS
HESTER KNIBBE HUNGERPOTS
MEL PRYOR SMALL NUCLEAR FAMILY
ELIZA STEFANIDI SLEEPING WITH PLATO
ELSPETH SMITH KEEPING BUSY
SAM EISENSTEIN TRAJECTORIES
TONY CHAN FOUR POINTS FOURTEEN LINES
MARIA APICHELLA PSALMODY
TERESE SVOBODA PROFESSOR HARRIMAN'S STEAM AIR-SHIP
ALICE ANDERSON THE WATERMARK
BEN PARKER THE AMAZING LOST MAN
MANDY KAHN MATH, HEAVEN, TIME

EYEWEAR PROSE

SUMIA SUKKAR THE BOY FROM ALEPPO WHO PAINTED THE WAR

EYEWEAR LITERARY CRITICISM

MARK FORD THIS DIALOGUE OF ONE - WINNER OF THE 2015 PEGASUS AWARD FOR POETRY CRITICISM FROM THE POETRY FOUNDATION (CHICAGO, USA).